Events

News for every

**The award-winning Fiat 127
is launched in April 1971.**

By Hugh Morrison

MONTPELIER PUBLISHING

Front cover (clockwise from left): Astronaut James Irwin on the moon. US President Richard Nixon. Malcolm McDowell as Alex in *A Clockwork Orange*. John Lennon and Yoko Ono.

Back cover (clockwise from top): Old London Bridge rebuilt in Arizona. Anti-Vietnam War protests in Washington DC. The Rolling Stones. Britain's new decimal coinage. The new British Leyland Morris Marina Coupe. Michael Caine in *Get Carter*.

Image credits: Jalo. David Hume Kennerly. Mark E. Anefo. Archives New Zealand. Edgar Mitchell/NASA. United States Geological Survey. Rob Croes/Anefo. Dave Gans. Martinra1966. Heinrich Klaffs. Hans Peters/Anefo. Bert Verhoeff/Anefo. Christopher Q. Stone. John Anderson. German Federal Archives. Jennifer L Johnson. Rhododendrites. Arpingstone. Avro. Leena A. Krohn. RVD/Jeroen van der Meyde. Herbert S. Gart. Kathy Reesey. Loco Steve. Duncan Hull. Louise Palanker. Jim Summaria. Craig O'Neal. Retroplum. Harald Krichel. MacKrys. Corpse Reviver. *Chicago Daily News.* Geoff Sheppard. Charles O'Rear. Michael Bulcik. Eva Rinaldi. Lawrence Lustig. Steve F. Karon Liu. Ingmar Runge. Thomas Nguyen. *Intel Free Press.* Sankat Oswell. National Archives of the United Arab Emirates. Rob Mieremet.

Published in Great Britain by Montpelier Publishing.
ISBN: 9798644284665

Events of 1971

News for every day of the year

January 1971

Friday 1: No-fault divorce becomes available in Britain.

The last cigarette advertisement airs on US TV at 11.50pm before a nationwide ban goes into effect.

Saturday 2: 66 people are killed in a stairway crush at the Ibrox football stadium in Glasgow, Scotland.

Sunday 3: The BBC begins its Open University broadcasts, enabling TV viewers to study for a degree at home.

Monday 4: Swedish diplomat Gunnar Jarring presents the results of his mission to settle the Arab-Israeli conflict.

Tuesday 5: The first one day international cricket match is played (England *v* Australia) in Melbourne, due to bad weather preventing a traditional three day Test match.

Wednesday 6: Eric Clapton's short lived band Derek and the Dominos, famous for the song *Layla*, makes their only TV appearance when they perform on *The Johnny Cash Show*.

Thursday 7: American horror writer Stephen King marries author Tabitha Spruce.

Left: Derek and the Dominos.

January 1971

George Harrison.

Carol O'Connor as Archie Bunker.

Friday 8: The British ambassador to Uruguay, Sir Jeffrey Jackson, is kidnapped by leftist guerillas and held hostage until September. It is later revealed that the British government pays £42,000 for his release.

Saturday 9: George Harrison's single *My Sweet Lord* enters the second of its three weeks at the top of the US charts.

Sunday 10: French fashion designer Coco Chanel dies aged 87.

Monday 11: The nickname 'Silicon Valley' for the computer manufacturing area of California is first used in print, in an article in *Electronic News.*

Tuesday 12: The TV sitcom *All in the Family* starring Carroll O'Connor as Archie Bunker is first broadcast. It is the US version of the BBC's *Til Death Us Do Part.*

Wednesday 13: British modernist composer Robert Still dies aged 60.

Thursday 14: Left wing extremist group The Angry Brigade admits responsibility for a bomb attack on the home of UK Employment Secretary Robert Carr on 12 January.

The first Commonwealth Heads of Government Conference to be held outside London opens in Singapore.

January 1971

Friday 15: Egypt's Aswan High Dam is officially opened.

Saturday 16: Ard Schenk of the Netherlands sets the world record for speed skating (1500m in 1.58.7).

Sunday 17: The Baltimore Colts win the US Superbowl, defeating the Dallas Cowboys 16-13 at Miami's Orange Bowl.

Monday 18: Northern Ireland Prime Minister James Chichester-Clark meets British Home Secretary Reginald Maudling to discuss joint action on rioting and disorder in the province.

Tuesday 19: The Beatles song *Helter Skelter* is played in court during the trial of serial killer Charles Manson, who claims that the lyrics inspired him to murder.

Wednesday 20: Gary Barlow, lead singer of Take That, is born in Cheshire, England.

Britain's first national postal strike begins, eventually lasting seven weeks.

Gary Barlow.

Ard Schenk: world record skater.

Thursday 21: Britain's tallest free-standing structure, the 1084 feet/330.4m tall Emley Moor TV mast in West Yorkshire, is declared open.

January 1971

Friday 22: The Singapore Declaration, outlining the principles of the new voluntary, revised British Commonwealth, is issued.

Saturday 23: The lowest ever temperature in the USA is recorded at Prospect Creek, Alaska (-80F/-62C).

Sunday 24: 58 people are sentenced to death in Africa's Republic of Guinea for their part in a failed Portuguese military coup in 1970.

Monday 25: Idi Amin becomes dictator of Uganda following a military coup.

Serial killer Charles Manson is found guilty of the murder of Sharon Tate and others in 1969.

**Above; The Bee Gees.
Below: Idi Amin.**

Tuesday 26: Seven people are killed in a flash flood in Canberra, Australia, after an estimated 3.7 inches/95 mm of rain falls in one hour.

Wednesday 27: Scotsman Dougal Robertson sets sail with his family on a round the world trip the yacht Lucette. In 1972 the family are shipwrecked for 38 days, inspiring the book and film *Survive the Savage Sea*.

Thursday 28: The Bee Gees record their first US number one hit, *How Can You Mend a Broken Heart?*

January 1971

Friday 29: BBC sports presenter Clare Balding is born in Kingsclere, Hampshire.

Australian fast bowler Dennis Keith Lillee MBE makes his Test cricket debut against England.

Saturday 30: Elvis Presley records his live album *Country Hero in Vegas* at the International Hotel, Las Vegas.

Sunday 31: Apollo 14, NASA's third successful lunar mission, is launched.

The crew of the Apollo 14 lunar mission (left to right):
Command Module pilot, Stuart A. Roosa, Commander, Alan B. Shepard
Jr. and Lunar Module pilot Edgar D. Mitchell.

February 1971

Monday 1: 1930s English dance-band leader Harry Roy dies aged 71.

Licences for domestic radio sets are abolished in the UK.

Tuesday 2: The Ramsar Convention on the international preservation of wetlands is signed.

Michael Caine in *Get Carter*.

Wednesday 3: British crime thriller *Get Carter* starring Michael Caine premieres in the USA.

Thursday 4: British luxury car manufacturer Rolls Royce goes bankrupt and is nationalised, remaining in state hands until 1987.

Friday 5: Apollo 14, piloted by Alan Shepherd, successfully lands on the moon.

Saturday 6: Gnr Robert Curtis, 20, of 156 Battery, Royal Artillery, becomes the first British soldier of 1,441 to be killed in the 38-year-long campaign in Northern Ireland known as 'The Troubles'.

Alan Shepherd raises the Stars and Stripes on the moon.

February 1971

Sunday 7: Switzerland votes in a referendum for nationwide women's suffrage.

Monday 8: New York's Nasdaq stock market, the world's first electronic stock exchange, goes into operation.

Tuesday 9: The Sylmar Earthquake hits Los Angeles, killing at least 50 people and causing major damage to buildings.

The Apollo 14 moon mission returns to Earth.

Wednesday 10: A total lunar eclipse takes place, visible over North America and Europe.

Thursday 11: The USA, UK and USSR sign the Seabed Treaty, prohibiting the use of nuclear weapons on the ocean floor.

Protestors in Amsterdam demonstrate against the invasion of Laos.

Friday 12: American businessman James Cash Penney, founder of the J.C. Penney department store chain, dies aged 95.

Saturday 13: South Vietnamese troops invade the neighbouring country of Laos, with US support.

Sunday 14: US President Richard Nixon installs a secret taping system in the White House; it is on this system that the Watergate tapes are recorded.

February 1971

Monday 15: The United Kingdom and the Republic of Ireland switch to decimal currency, ending the centuries old system of 12 pence in a shilling and twenty shillings in a pound.

Tuesday 16: Canada's Prime Minister Pierre Trudeau is accused of mouthing obscenities at opposition MPs in Parliament; he later claims he only said 'fuddle duddle'.

Wednesday 17: England's cricket team captained by Ray Illingworth wins The Ashes series after beating Australia in the seventh Test.

Thursday 18: Pop artist Andy Warhol attends the opening of a major exhibition of his works at London's Tate Gallery.

Friday 19: British prog-rock band Yes release their third album, *The Yes Album.*

A presentation pack showing the UK's old and new coins. On 15 February the British and Irish pound switch from 240 to 100 pennies in the pound. The value of the pound itself does not change.

February 1971

Saturday 20: The early warning message for a nuclear attack is accidentally broadcast on all US radio stations. Some stations go off the air but many ignore it.

Sunday 21: 123 people are killed in a series of 19 tornadoes which hit the state of Mississippi.

David Crosby.

Monday 22: David Crosby, formerly of Crosby, Stills and Nash releases his first solo album, *If Only I Could Remember My Name.*

Tuesday 23: British glamour model and TV presenter Melinda Messenger is born in Swindon, Wiltshire.

Melinda Messenger is born on 23 February.

Wednesday 24: Several countries object to the UK's Immigration Bill which proposes to reduce non-white Commonwealth immigration.

Thursday 25: A partial (78%) solar eclipse takes place across much of the eastern hemisphere.

Friday 26: Two RUC officers are shot dead by IRA gunmen while on patrol in Belfast, Northern Ireland.

Saturday 27: British TV illusionist Derren Brown is born in Purley, Surrey.

Sunday 28: Stunt motorcyclist Evel Knieval jumps over a record 19 cars at the Ontario Motor Speedway, California.

March 1971

Monday 1: Luciano Visconti's film *Death in Venice*, starring Dirk Bogarde, receives its royal premiere in London. The proceeds are donated to the Venice in Peril fund.

Tuesday 2: British comedian Dave Gorman is born in Stafford.

The scientific sceptic Samuel Shenton, founder of the Flat Earth Society, dies aged 67.

Wednesday 3: A severe three day blizzard hits Canada, with 17 inches/43 cm of snow falling on Montreal, the biggest fall on record until 2012.

Thursday 4: The 24th British Academy Film Awards are presented in London. *Butch Cassidy and the Sundance Kid* wins Best Film.

Friday 5: Led Zeppelin perform *Stairway to Heaven* live for the first time, in a concert in Belfast, Northern Ireland.

Saturday 6: Extreme cold weather hits Italy, with a record low temperature of -30F (-34.6C) in the Italian Alps.

Robert Plant and Jimmy Page of Led Zeppelin.

March 1971

Sunday 7: Britain's first postal strike ends after 47 days.

Boxer Joe Frazier jokes with reporters after his defeat of Muhammed Ali.

Monday 8: Boxer Joe Frazier defeats Muhammed Ali at Madison Square Garden, New York.

Comedian Harold Lloyd, shown here in 1924, dies on 8 March.

Silent comedy film star Harold Lloyd dies aged 77.

Tuesday 9: Pope Cyril VI of Alexandria, primate of the Coptic church, dies aged 68.

Wednesday 10: Three unarmed off-duty British soldiers, aged 17, 18 and 23, are killed by IRA gunmen in Belfast. It is the first time off-duty soldiers have been killed in the province.

Thursday 11: Following a public outcry over the murder of three unarmed British servicemen in Belfast, Home Secretary Reginald Maudlin raises the minimum age of troops engaging in Northern Ireland to 18, and states 'the battle now joined against the terrorists will be fought with the utmost vigour and determination.'

March 1971

Friday 12: Turkey's prime minister Suleyman Demirel is ousted in a military coup.

Saturday 13: Wales beat Ireland 23-9 to win the 1971 Five Nations rugby tournament in Cardiff, Wales.

Sunday 14: Australia's Ken Rosewall beats Arthur Ashe of the USA to win the Australian Mens' Tennis Open tournament.

Monday 15: Mrs Indira Ghandi is re-elected as Prime Minister of India.

Tuesday 16: Trygve Batelli becomes Prime Minister of Norway.

Ken Roswall.

Wednesday 17: Welsh comedian and singer Sir Harry Secombe opens the newly restored London Welsh Centre in Gray's Inn Road, London.

Eddie Merckx.

Thursday 18: Singer Peter Gabriel of Genesis marries Jill Moore, daughter of HM the Queen's private secretary Lord Moore of Wolvercote.

Friday 19: Cyclist Eddie Merckx wins the Milan-Sanremo race for the fourth time.

Saturday 20: The Prime Minister of Northern Ireland, James Chichester-Clark, resigns after his request for more troops to quell disorder in the province is refused by UK Home Secretary James Callaghan.

The Westland Lynx helicopter.

Sunday 21: The record-breaking British military helicopter the Westland Lynx makes its first flight.

Brian Faulkner.

Monday 22: Brian Faulkner becomes the last Prime Minister of Northern Ireland. The office becomes defunct in 1972 when the UK imposes direct rule.

Tuesday 23: British film director Basil Dearden, 60, (*The Blue Lamp, Pool of London, Victim*), is killed in a car crash on Westway, London. In an odd twist, his final film, *The Man Who Haunted Himself*, is about a man killed in an accident on the same road.

Wednesday 24: The International Patent Classification is set up to standardise the patent system in most countries.

Thursday 25: The Pakistani army begins Operation Searchlight to crush nationalist uprising in East Pakistan (now Bangladesh).

Friday 26: East Pakistan declares independence in a radio broadcast from Chittagong.

Saturday 27: Wales wins the Five Nations rugby tournament when it defeats France 9-5 at Stade de Colombes, Paris.

March 1971

Sunday 28: The final episode of the popular Second World War TV comedy *Hogan's Heroes* is broadcast.

Monday 29: Lt William Calley, US Army, is found guilty of the murder of 22 South Vietnamese civilians in the My Lai Massacre of 1969. He is sentenced to life imprisonment but released in 1976 after a public outcry.

Tuesday 30: British naturalist and war artist Richard Talbot Kelly MBE MC dies aged 74.

The first Starbucks coffee shop opens in Seattle, Washington.

Wednesday 31: Actor Ewan McGregor (*Trainspotting, Star Wars*) is born in Perth, Scotland.

**The first branch of Starbucks, at 1912 Pike Place, Seattle, WA.
Originally at 2000 Western Avenue, the shop moves here in 1976.**

April 1971

Thursday 1: Restrictions on private ownership of gold bullion and coins are lifted in the UK.

Friday 2: The British parliament discusses amendments to the Marriage Act 1949 in light of 'sex-change' surgery developments.

Saturday 3: Monaco wins the Eurovision Song Contest with *Un Banc, un Arbre, un Rue* by Séverine.

Prolific crime writer Manfred B. Lee, who wrote under the pseudonym Ellery Queen, dies aged 66.

Sunday 4: The USSR launches Kosmos 404, an anti-satellite missile, which shoots down the previously launched Kosmos 400 satellite in a weapons test.

Monday 5: A major eruption of Sicily's Mount Etna begins.

West German leader Willy Brandt meets British Prime Minister Edward Heath for talks on joining the EEC (later EU).

Russian composer Igor Stravinsky dies on 6 April.

Tuesday 6: Russian composer Igor Stravinsky dies aged 88.

Wednesday 7: US President Richard Nixon makes a live nationwide TV broadcast in which he pledges to withdraw 100,000 troops from Vietnam in the coming year.

Thursday 8: The 1971 Masters golf tournament opens in Augusta, Georgia.

West German leader Willy Brandt.

April 1971

Portrait of the serial killer Charles Manson.

Friday 9: Serial killer Charles Manson is sentenced to death for his role in the murder of Sharon Tate and others in 1969; it is later commuted to life imprisonment.

Saturday 10: Independence fighters in Mujibnagar, East Pakistan, form the first provisional government of Bangladesh.

Sunday 11: Charles Coody wins the 1971 Masters golf tournament, beating Johnny Miller and Jack Nicklaus by two shots.

Monday 12: Dutch Formula one motorcyclist Edwin Straver dies aged 48 following injuries sustained during a race in January.

Tuesday 13: Former Beatle John Lennon records the song *God Save Oz*, a fundraising record for the publishers of *Oz* magazine, recently charged with obscenity.

Wednesday 14: The Djoudj National Bird Sanctuary is established in Senegal.

Thursday 15: London's Barbican Centre cultural complex is granted planning permission.

Friday 16: The Rolling Stones release their hit single *Brown Sugar*.

Sheikh Mujibur Rhaman.

Saturday 17: British singer Claire Sweeney is born in Liverpool.

The People's Republic of Bangladesh (formerly East Pakistan) is officially formed under Sheikh Mujibur Rahman.

April 1971

The Rolling Stones advertise their new album, *Sticky Fingers*.

Sunday 18: British actor David Tennant (*Dr Who*) is born in Bathgate, West Lothian.

London's Kentish Town West railway station is destroyed by fire. It does not reopen until 1981.

Monday 19: The USSR launches the world's first space station, Salyut 1, into orbit.

Tuesday 20: The US Supreme Court rules that bussing (compulsory racial integration in schools) is not unconstitutional.

Dr Who star David Tennant is born on 18 April.

Wednesday 21: Francois 'Papa Doc' Duvalier, President of Haiti, dies aged 64; his son Jean-Claude 'Baby Doc' Duvalier succeeds as President for life.

Thursday 22: The Rolling Stones' album *Sticky Fingers* is released.

Friday 23: The USSR launches Soyuz 10 to dock with newly launched space station Salyut 1.

April 1971

Saturday 24: Large protests against US involvement in the Vietnam War take place in San Francisco and Washington, DC.

Sunday 25: Todor Zhivkov is re-elected as de-facto dictator of Bulgaria.

Monday 26: A state of emergency is declared in Turkey following violent nationwide demonstrations.

Tuesday 27: British Leyland launches the Morris Marina saloon car, a replacement for the popular Morris Minor, in production since 1948.

Wednesday 28: Samuel L Gravely Jr becomes the first black admiral in the US Navy; he was also the first black officer in the service and the first to captain a ship engaged in combat.

The Morris Marina.

Thursday 29: The Piper PA-48 prop fighter, based on the famous Mustang of the Second World War era, makes its first test flight in the USA.

Friday 30: Dublin band Thin Lizzy release their debut album, *Thin Lizzy.*

Thin Lizzy (left to right): Brian Downey, Phil Lynott, Gary Moore.

May 1971

Saturday 1: The quasi-public US rail service Amtrak goes into operation.

A bomb planted by left-wing terror group The Angry Brigade explodes in the Biba fashion store in Kensington, London.

Sunday 2: Leftist guerillas launch a series of attacks on public buildings in Sri Lanka.

Monday 3: In Washington, DC, 12,000 people are arrested in May Day protests against the war in Vietnam.

Anti-war protestors, including veterans, march in Washington DC.

Tuesday 4: The British Parliament discusses proposals for a third London airport at Foulness; the plans are never approved.

Wednesday 5: Violet Jessop, famous for surviving the sinking of both the RMS *Titanic* and the HMS *Britannic* in 1916, dies aged 83.

Thursday 6: British 1950s pop star Dickie Valentine dies aged 41 in a car crash near Crickhowell, Wales.

May 1971

Friday 7: Britain's Labour Party announces it has adopted a neutral stance on the country's proposed membership of the European Economic Community (EEC; later EU).

Saturday 8: Arsenal beats Liverpool 2-1 at Wembley Stadium to win the FA Cup Final. It is the first Cup Final in which a substitute scores a goal.

Sunday 9: NASA's Mariner 8 probe is launched on a Mars mission but fails to enter orbit.

Monday 10: Swedish model Agneta Freiberg, 25, one of the first supermodels, dies after injuries sustained in a fall from a balcony in Paris on 6 February.

Britain's *Daily Sketch*, in print since 1909, merges with the relaunched *Daily Mail* in a joint edition on 12 May.

Tuesday 11: Britain's oldest tabloid newspaper, the *Daily Sketch*, ceases publication after 62 years.

Wednesday 12: Mick Jagger marries Bianca de Macias in Saint-Tropez, France, in an RC church service attended by Paul McCartney and Ringo Starr.

Thursday 13: The state funeral takes place in Dublin of the former Prime Minister of the Republic of Ireland, Sean Lemass, who died on 11 May.

Friday 14: The Pink Floyd compilation album *Relics* is released in the UK.

May 1971

Sean Lemass, former Irish PM, dies on 11 May.

Saturday 15: The Israeli Consul General in Turkey, Ephraim Elrom, is kidnapped and murdered by terrorists linked to the Palestinian Liberation Organisation (PLO).

Sunday 16: The Benjamin Britten opera *Owen Wingrave,* recorded in Aldeburgh in 1970, premieres on BBC TV.

Monday 17: Her Majesty Queen Maxima, Queen Consort of the Netherlands, is born in Buenos Aires, Argentina.

Peter Pears stars as Gen. Sir Philip Wingrave in Benjamin Britten's opera *Owen Wingrave.*

Tuesday 18: Elizabeth Anne Porteus, 33, a high school teacher, is found dead at her home in Alberta, Canada. She is later identified as the final victim of Wayne Boden, the notorious 'Vampire Rapist'.

Wednesday 19: American poet and humourist Ogden Nash dies aged 68.

Thursday 20: In soccer, Chelsea beats Real Madrid 2-1 to gain the European Cup Winners' Cup.

The Boeing SST (Supersonic Transport) project, America's answer to *Concorde*, is scrapped.

May 1971

British Formula One racing champion Jackie Stewart (shown here in 1969) wins the 1971 Monaco Grand Prix on 23 May.

Friday 21: Serious rioting breaks out among angry fans after singer Wilson Pickett cancels a concert in Chatanooga, Tennessee, eventually requiring National Guard troops to restore order.

Saturday 22: Over 1000 people are killed in a 20-second earthquake in Bingol, Turkey.

Don McLean: he records *American Pie* on 26 May.

Sunday 23: British racing driver Jackie Stewart wins the 1971 Monaco Grand Prix.

78 people, mostly British tourists, are killed in a plane crash near Rijeka Airport in Yugoslavia.

Monday 24: Hurricane Agatha hits Mexico.

Tuesday 25: Sergeant Michael Willetts, 27, of 3rd Btn the Parachute Regiment, is fatally wounded while shielding two children from an IRA terrorist's bomb in Belfast; for this action he is awarded the George Cross posthumously.

May 1971

Wednesday 26: American folk singer Don McLean records his hit song *American Pie.*

Thursday 27: 46 people are killed in a rail crash at Dahlerau, West Germany.

Friday 28: The USSR launches the Mars 3 probe.

Saturday 29: Al Unser wins the Indianapolis 500 motor race for the second year in succession.

Sunday 30: NASA launches the Mariner 9 Mars rocket.

Monday 31: The city of Madison, Wisconsin, cancels its Memorial Day Parade, instead holding a day of mourning and repentance for the Vietnam War.

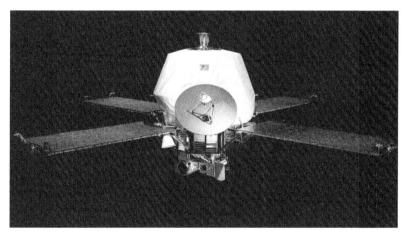

The Mariner 9 Mars probe.

June 1971

Tuesday 1: The musical *You're a Good Man Charlie Brown*, based on Charles M Schulz's Peanuts cartoons, opens on Broadway.

Wednesday 2: AFC Ajax of The Netherlands defeats Panathinakos FC of Greece 2-0 in the European Cup soccer final at Wembley Stadium, London.

Evonne Goolagong.

Thursday 3: One of the longest running British stage shows, the comedy *No Sex Please We're British* starring Michael Crawford opens at London's Strand Theatre. Despite being disliked by critics, it plays to full houses until 1987.

Friday 4: The USSR launches the Kosmos 426 satellite to study the Earth's upper atmosphere.

Saturday 5: Singer and actor Mark Wahlberg is born in Boston, Massachusetts.

Mark Wahlberg: born on 5 June.

Evonne Goolagong defeats Helen Gourlay (both of Australia) to win the French Open Women's Singles tennis title.

Sunday 6: The final edition of *The Ed Sullivan Show* is broadcast in the USA. The variety programme enjoyed a 23 year run and is probably best known for bringing The Beatles to the attention of the American public.

Monday 7: The USSR's Soyuz 11 rocket, launched on 6 June, becomes the first craft to dock with a space station when it reaches Salyut 1.

June 1971

Tuesday 8: Singer David Bowie begins recording on his album *Hunky Dory.*

Wednesday 9: Actor Harold Lloyd Jr, 40, son of the silent comedian Harold Lloyd, dies from a stroke just three months after his father.

Thursday 10: British actor Michael Rennie (*The Day the Earth Stood Still*) dies aged 61.

Graffitti from the 1971 occupation of Alcatraz.

Friday 11: The 19 month long civil rights protest occupation of the unused Alcatraz prison island by 89 American Indians comes to an end.

British dance band leader Bert Ambrose dies aged 74.

Saturday 12: The British weekly children's comic *Knockout* is first published by IPC Magazines. It merges with *Whizzer and Chips* in 1973.

Sunday 13: The *New York Times* begins publishing a series of leaked documents known as the Pentagon Papers which discredit the US government's role in the Vietnam War.

Monday 14: The first Hard Rock Cafe opens in London; it begins worldwide expansion in 1982.

British Education Secretary Margaret Thatcher announces plans to end taxpayer-funded milk for schoolchildren.

Tuesday 15: The first large scale production of Norwegian oil from the North Sea begins.

June 1971

Wednesday 16: The American rapper Tupac Shakur is born in New York City (died 1996).

Thursday 17: The US government agrees to hand back control of the Okinawa islands, occupied since 1945, to Japan.

Friday 18: Southwest Airlines begins operation in the USA.

Saturday 19: US speedboat racer Garfield Wood, the first man to travel at over 100 mph on water, dies aged 90.

Sunday 20: The British government announces that the defecting Soviet space scientist Anatoli Fedoseyev has been granted asylum.

Monday 21: Britain begins new negotiations to enter the European Economic Community (EEC, later EU).

Tuesday 22: Soviet submarine B-427 is launched. It goes on to become a floating museum at Long Beach, California, after the end of the Cold War.

Wednesday 23: The motor racing film *Le Mans* starring Steve McQueen is released.

Thursday 24: The EEC (later the European Union) agrees terms for Britain's membership.

The crew of Soyuz 11 killed on 30 June: (l-r) Georgy Dobrovolsky, Vladislav Volkov and Viktor Patsayev.

June 1971

Friday 25: The first Reading Festival takes place, featuring jazz, blues and rock, at Reading in Berkshire, England.

Saturday 26: Spanish composer Juan Manen dies aged 88.

Sunday 27: New York City's famous Fillmore East music venue closes. Opened in 1925, it hosted acts including Jimi Hendrix, Led Zeppelin and the Grateful Dead.

Elon Musk, founder of Tesla, is born on 28 June.

Monday 28: Entrepreneur Elon Musk, founder of Tesla, is born in Johannesburg, South Africa.

Tuesday 29: A two-day cricket match between Lancashire and Pakistan at Old Trafford ends in a draw.

Wednesday 30: All three crew of the USSR's Soyuz 11 space station mission are found dead when their landing craft reaches Earth, most likely caused by a faulty air supply in their cabin.

July 1971

Jim Morrison: found dead on 3 July.

Thursday 1: The semi-autonomous United States Postal Service (USPS) goes into operation. Previously, mail was handled by a government department, the US Post Office.

Friday 2: The Royal Scots Dragoon Guards is formed from an amalgamation of three cavalry regiments.

Saturday 3: Jim Morrison, 27, lead singer of The Doors, is found dead in his apartment in Paris. The cause of death is never established.

Sunday 4: The UK's Jackie Stewart wins the French Grand Prix.

Poet and critic Sir Maurice Bowra, Vice-Chancellor of Oxford University, dies aged 73.

Monday 5: The 26th Amendment to the US Constitution lowers the legal voting age from 21 to 18.

Louis Armstrong dies on 6 July.

Tuesday 6: Jazz trumpeter and singer Louis Armstrong (*Wonderful World*) dies aged 69.

Three French tourists are found shot dead on a campsite in Cheshire, England, in an apparently motiveless attack.

Wednesday 7: Cartoonist and animator Ub Iwerks, co-creator with Walt Disney of Mickey Mouse, dies aged 70.

July 1971

Corey Feldman is born on 16 July.

Thursday 8: Two rioters are shot dead by British troops in Londonderry, Northern Ireland.

Friday 9: 25,000 people attend the funeral of jazz legend Louis Armstrong in New York City; the Lord's Prayer is sung by Peggy Lee at the service.

Saturday 10: A failed coup begins in Morocco as troops storm the royal palace during birthday celebrations for HM King Hassan II.

Sunday 11: Mexican racing driver Pedro Rodriquez, 31, is killed during the Interserie race at Nuremberg, Germany.

Monday 12: British soldier Private David Walker, 30, Royal Greenjackets, is shot dead by an IRA sniper on Northumberland Street, Belfast.

Tuesday 13: Michael Basset, 24, is found dead of asphyxiation in his car near Barlaston, Staffordshire. Police find a note confessing to the murder of three French tourists in Cheshire on 6 July. His motive for the killings is never established.

Wednesday 14: Private Richard Barton, 24, of 2nd Battalion The Parachute Regiment, is killed in an IRA ambush in Anderstown, Belfast.

Thursday 15: Anglo-Irish theatre director Sir Tyrone Guthrie dies aged 70.

Friday 16: Actor Corey Feldman (*Stand by Me, The Goonies*) is born in Reseda, California.

Saturday 17: British racing driver Jackie Stewart wins the 1971 British Grand Prix at Silverstone.

July 1971

Sunday 18: The former British Trucial State protectorates of the Persian Gulf, including Dubai and Abu Dhabi, agree to form the United Arab Emirates.

Monday 19: The south tower of New York City's World Trade Center is completed.

Tuesday 20: Canadian actress and Bond girl Sandra Oh (*Grey's Anatomy*) is born in Nepean, Ontario.

Wednesday 21: George Klippert, the last Canadian to be imprisoned for homosexual acts, is released from jail.

Thursday 22: A communist coup in the African state of the Sudan is defeated after three days.

Friday 23: The southern extension of London Underground's Victoria Line, from Victoria to Brixton, is opened by HRH Princess Alexandra.

The crew of Apollo 15 during rocket preparations.

Hasbro launches the Weeble toy, a small egg shaped doll.

Saturday 24: Belgian driver Raymond Mathay is killed during the 24 Hours of Spa rally in Belgium.

Sunday 25: The Japanese missionary David Tsutada, known as the 'John Wesley of Japan' who was imprisoned for his Christian beliefs during the Second World War, dies aged 65.

July 1971

Monday 26: The Apollo 15 moon rocket is launched.

Tuesday 27: British explorer Sir Ranulph Fiennes ends his military service in the army of the Sultanate of Oman.

Wednesday 28: The motorcycle racing documentary film *On Any Sunday,* featuring Steve McQueen, is launched in the USA.

Thursday 29: The British Black Arrow space rocket programme is cancelled.

Friday 30: 162 people are killed when an All Nippon Airways flight crashes near Shizukuishi, Japan.

The Apollo 15 crew touches down on the moon.

Saturday 31: The crew of Apollo 15 become the first astronauts to use a Lunar Rover vehicle.

Apollo 15 astronaut Jim Irwin with the Lunar Rover.

August 1971

Sunday 1: 40,000 people attend George Harrison's fundraising Concert for Bangladesh in New York City.

Monday 2: Ruth Lawrence, the child prodigy who gains a First in mathematics at Oxford University aged 13, is born in Brighton, England.

Tuesday 3: Former Beatle Paul McCartney announces the formation of his new group, Wings.

Wednesday 4: The novelist and writer Denis MacKail, best known for his biography of 'Peter Pan' creator J.M. Barrie, dies aged 79.

Thursday 5: The Prime Minister of the UK, Edward Heath, agrees with the Prime Minister of Northern Ireland, Brian Faulkner, to introduce internment (imprisonment without trial) for suspected IRA terrorists.

Friday 6: A total lunar eclipse lasting one hour and 40 minutes is observed over Africa, Asia and parts of Australia and South America.

Paul and Linda McCartney of Wings.

August 1971

British yachtsman Sir Charles (Chay) Blyth becomes the first person to sail solo around the world westwards.

Saturday 7: The Apollo 15 moon rocket returns to Earth safely, despite one of its three parachutes failing to function.

Sunday 8: France performs a nuclear bomb test at Mururoa Atoll in the Pacific.

Monday 9: Riots break out in Northern Ireland as mass internment of IRA suspects begins.

Tuesday 10: *Mr Tickle*, the first of Roger Hargreaves' series of *Mr Men* children's books is published.

Wednesday 11: Britain wins the Admiral's Cup international yacht race, with one of the boats skippered by the Prime Minister, Edward Heath.

Thursday 12: The Ukraine's Faina Melnik breaks the world record for women's shot putt with a throw of 64.22 metres (210.6 feet) at the European Athletics Championships in Helsinki, Finland.

**Above: Pete Sampras, born on 13 August.
Below: Faina Melnik.**

Friday 13: Tennis champion Pete Sampras is born in Washington, D.C.

Saturday 14: Bahrain declares independence from the United Kingdom.

The Who release their album *Who's Next.*

Sunday 15: In an attempt to cover the cost of the Vietnam War and the space programme, the US government takes the dollar permanently off the gold standard. A 90 day freeze on wage, rent and retail price increases is also announced.

August 1971

Monday 16: The US dollar falls sharply in the world currency markets following its departure from the gold standard; American tourists in London receive up to 20% less sterling in exchange.

Tuesday 17: At least 90 people are killed when Typhoon Rose hits Hong Kong with winds of 130mph.

The USS *Regulus* is grounded in Hong Kong harbour following Typhoon Rose.

Wednesday 18: The governments of Australia and New Zealand announce the withdrawal of their troops from Vietnam by the end of the year.

Thursday 19: The first match of soccer's 1971/72 European Cup takes place; Spain's Valencia defeats Union Luxembourg 3-1 at home.

Friday 20: 1000 gallons of oil are spilled on President Nixon's private beach at San Clemente, California, by the USS *Manatee.*

Saturday 21: Bank robber and 'Black Panther' activist George Jackson is shot dead by guards after killing five men in a dramatic escape attempt from California's Soledad prison.

Sunday 22: The FBI arrests a group of anti-war protestors including five clergymen known as the Camden 28 who were attempting to destroy records in the draft office at Camden, New Jersey.

Monday 23: An unarmed policeman, Superintendent Gerry Richardson, 39, is shot dead in Blackpool, England following a jewellery shop raid. One of the most senior British police officers to be killed in the line of duty, Richardson is posthumously awarded the George Cross for gallantry.

Tuesday 24: A historic day for cricket as India beats the English side in their first Test victory on English soil.

Wednesday 25: The 32nd Venice International Film Festival opens.

Thursday 26: Actress and singer Thalia Sodi, 'The Queen of Latin Pop' is born in Mexico City, Mexico.

Friday 27: Five US soldiers are killed in an ambush in Danang, South Vietnam.

Saturday 28: Following the US dollar's departure from the gold standard, the Japanese Yen is allowed to float against the dollar for the first time.

Thalia Sodi: born 26 August.

Sunday 29: Corporal Ian Armstrong, 14/20th King's Hussars, is killed in an IRA ambush near Cullaville, County Armagh, Northern Ireland.

Monday 30: The Progressive Conservatives led by Peter Lougheed are victorious in the general election held in Alberta, Canada.

Tuesday 31: Australia's Adrienne Beames becomes the first woman to run a marathon in under three hours (2:46:30).

September 1971

Britain's 3d (three old pence) coin is withdrawn from circulation on 1 September.

Wednesday 1: Britain's 'thruppeny bit' (three old pence) coins cease to be legal tender.

Thursday 2: New tennis players Chris Evert and Jimmy Connors win their first matches at the US Open at Forest Hills.

Friday 3: Qatar becomes independent from the United Kingdom.

Former Beatle John Lennon leaves the UK for the USA, never to return.

Saturday 4: 111 people are killed when Alaska Airlines Flight 1866 crashes into a mountain near Juneau, Alaska.

Sunday 5: The director of the USA's Cost of Living Council states that the 90 day freeze on wage and price increases may have to be extended for 3-4 years.

Martin Freeman.

Monday 6: The 6th Jerry Lewis Muscular Dystrophy Telethon on US TV raises over eight million dollars.

Tuesday 7: The death toll in Northern Ireland reaches 100 as a 14 year-old girl is killed in crossfire between the IRA and British soldiers in Belfast.

Wednesday 8: British actor Martin Freeman (*The Hobbit, The Office*) is born in Aldershot, Hampshire.

September 1971

Thursday 9: A four day riot begins at the maximum-security state prison at Attica, New York.

Geoffrey Jackson, Britain's Ambassador to Uruguay is freed after being held captive by leftist guerillas for eight months.

Friday 10: The Bell 309 King Cobra helicopter makes its first flight.

Saturday 11: Thieves dig down into the vault of Lloyd's Bank in Baker Street, London, stealing an estimated £3m worth of property from safety deposit boxes. Police arrest the gang in October.

Above: Goran Ivanišević.

Former Soviet premier Nikita Kruschev dies aged 77.

Sunday 12: Stan Smith of the USA wins the US Open men's tennis final at Forest Hills, New York.

Monday 13: 10 people are killed and 70 injured in a catastrophic 200-vehicle pile-up during thick fog on Thelwall Viaduct near Manchester, England. It is the worst UK crash to this date.

Tennis player Goran Ivanišević, is born in Split, Yugoslavia (now Croatia).

Tuesday 14: Soviet scientists announce a method of creating cognac in 15 days instead of three years, using radiation.

Peter Falk as Columbo.

Wednesday 15: Following its successful 1968 pilot, the crime series *Columbo* starring Peter Falk is first broadcast on NBC TV.

September 1971

Thursday 16: The US photo-magazine *Look*, a competitor of *Life* magazine, ceases publication after 34 years.

Friday 17: ITV airs the first episode of *The Persuaders*, the glamorous action series starring Roger Moore and Tony Curtis.

Saturday 18: The first instant pot noodle snack, Cup Noodle, is launched by Nissin Foods of Japan.

Sunday 19: The UK's Jackie Stewart wins the Canadian Grand Prix at Mosport Park.

Monday 20: General George Forsyth announces that the US Army cannot end conscription before 1973.

Tuesday 21: The cult musical programme *The Old Grey Whistle Test* is first broadcast on BBC TV.

Wednesday 22: Nineties teen pop idol Chesney Hawkes is born in Slough, Berkshire, England.

The Emperor and Empress of Japan meet President and Mrs Nixon on 26 September.

September 1971

Detail from *The Love Letter*, stolen on 23 September.

Thursday 23: The 17th century Dutch genre painting *The Love Letter* by Jan Vermeer is stolen from the Centre for Fine Arts, Brussels. The thief is apprehended in October; the severely damaged painting requires extensive restoration.

Friday 24: Britain expels 90 Soviet diplomats on spying charges.

Saturday 25: Yugoslavia and the USSR sign an accord guaranteeing Yugoslavia's independence from Soviet influence.

Sunday 26: Emperor Hirohito becomes the first Japanese emperor to travel abroad, meeting US President Nixon for talks in Alaska.

The 'free town' or microstate of Christiania is founded in a 19-acre disused barracks in Copenhagen, Denmark.

Monday 27: Tripartite talks between the Prime Ministers of Great Britain, Northern Ireland and the Republic of Ireland take place at Chequers, England.

Tuesday 28: Cardinal József Mindszenty, former leader of the Roman Catholic church in Hungary, is allowed to leave US Embassy in Budapest, where he has sought refuge since the failed uprising against the Soviets in 1956.

Wednesday 29: An estimated 10,000 people are killed when a cyclone hits the Indian state of Orissa.

Thursday 30: The Washington Senators play their last game in their home town before moving to Texas. Large crowds storm the pitch after play, and the first base is stolen by a souvenir hunter.

October 1971

Friday 1: The 39 square mile Walt Disney World theme park opens in Bay Lake, Florida.

Saturday 2: The restored steam locomotive *King George V* begins a series of steam specials on British railways. The last scheduled steam service ended in 1968.

British Rail's Class 42 engines are withdrawn on 5 October.

Sunday 3: France's Francois Cevert wins the US Grand Prix motor race; the UK's Jackie Stewart wins the Formula One season overall on points.

Monday 4: Anti-war protestor and 'flower power' leader Abbie Hoffman announces that long hair on men is no longer an act of rebellion but has become an affectation.

Gene Hackman stars in *The French Connection,* released on 7 October.

Tuesday 5: The Class 42 'Warship' diesel locomotive ends its service on British Railways.

Wednesday 6: Operation Jefferson Glenn, the US Army's last major infantry offensive of the Vietnam War, is ended. US troops withdraw from Vietnam in 1973.

Thursday 7: The action thriller film *The French Connection,* starring Gene Hackman, is released in the USA.

October 1971

Old London Bridge re-opens in the Arizona desert on 10 October as part of a holiday resort.

Friday 8: John Lennon releases his hit single *Imagine.*

Saturday 9: Japan's Emperor Hirohito visits the Netherlands. His visit is met by protests over Japanese aggression in the Dutch East Indies in the Second World War.

Sunday 10: The long-running British TV series *Upstairs Downstairs* is broadcast for the first time.

Old London Bridge, transported from London to the USA brick by brick, re-opens in Lake Havasu City, Arizona.

Monday 11: Silent film comedian Chester Conklin, star of Mack Sennett's *Keystone Kops* series, dies aged 85.

Sascha Baron Cohen is born on 13 October.

Tuesday 12: The rock and roll star Gene Vincent, (*Be-Bop-A-Lu-La*), dies aged 36.

Wednesday 13: The British comedian Sascha Baron Cohen (Borat, Ali G) is born in Hammersmith, London.

Thursday 14: Ted Walters, 58, a veteran gangster who had links to notorious 1930s outlaws Bonnie and Clyde, is shot dead by police during a kidnap attempt in Euless, Texas.

October 1971

US Vice President Spiro Agnew.

Friday 15: British gambling magnate William Hill, founder of the betting shop chain of the same name, dies aged 68.

Saturday 16: US Vice President Spiro Agnew makes a state visit to his ancestral homeland of Greece.

Sunday 17: Britain's Prime Minister Edward Heath orders an immediate enquiry into allegations by a London newspaper that IRA suspects in Northern Ireland have been subjected to torture.

Monday 18: The Knapp Commission begins an investigation into police corruption in New York City. The resulting scandal is later dramatised in the film *Serpico* starring Al Pacino.

Tuesday 19: The USSR launches the Kosmos 453 anti-ballistic missile satellite.

An amendment in the US Congress to end the war in Vietnam is defeated by 23 votes.

Dannii Minogue is born on 20 October.

Wednesday 20: The singer and actress Dannii Minogue, sister of Kylie Minogue, is born in Melbourne, Australia.

West Germany's Chancellor Willy Brandt is awarded the Nobel Peace Prize, the first time it has been won by a head of state for 50 years.

Thursday 21: 20 people are killed in a gas explosion in Clarkston, East Renfrewshire, Scotland.

October 1971

Friday 22: Over 40 appliances are required to fight a huge fire at the historic Texas Mill in Ashton-Under-Lyne, near Manchester, England. One fireman is killed in the blaze.

British boxing champion Audley Harrison MBE is born on 26 October.

Saturday 23: The Romanian serial killer Ion Rimaru, known as the 'Vampire of Bucharest', is executed by firing squad. In a strange twist, Rimaru's father Florea is later discovered to have been a serial killer in the 1940s.

Sunday 24: Mr Harry Drake, 56, of Nevada, breaks the world archery record by shooting an arrow 2,028 yards (1854m).

Monday 25: The United Nations General Assembly expels the Republic of China (the remaining capitalist portion of China known as Taiwan) and admits the communist Peoples' Republic of China in its place.

Tuesday 26: Audley Harrison MBE, the European heavyweight boxing champion and Olympic gold medalist, is born in London, England.

Wednesday 27: The Democratic Republic of the Congo is renamed Zaire.

Dr Gerard Newe OBE becomes the first Roman Catholic to serve as a minister of state in the Government of Northern Ireland.

Thursday 28: Britain's House of Commons votes 356-244 in favour of joining the European Economic Community. This later becomes the European Union (EU).

October 1971

London's Post Office Tower.

Friday 29: Actress Winona Ryder is born in Olmstead, Minnesota.

US troop numbers in Vietnam reach their lowest level since 1966.

Saturday 30: The Reverend Ian Paisley founds his Democratic Unionist Party in Northern Ireland.

Sunday 31: A bomb, thought to be planted by the IRA, explodes in the revolving restaurant on top of London's Post Office Tower (now the BT Tower). Following the attack the tower is largely closed to the public.

November 1971

Monday 1: Two police officers are killed and 12 people injured during bomb attacks and civil disorder in Belfast, Northern Ireland.

Tuesday 2: Queen Elizabeth II attends the State Opening of Parliament, vowing in her speech that the government will stop bloodshed in Northern Ireland.

Wednesday 3: The thriller *Play Misty For Me,* starring Clint Eastwood, is released in the USA.

Thursday 4: Mrs Emma Groves, 51, is blinded by a rubber bullet fired by an unidentified British soldier following disturbances during house-to-house searches in Belfast. She afterwards begins a campaign to ban the use of the bullets by the army.

Friday 5: Elton John's fourth studio album, *Madman Across The Water,* is released.

Saturday 6: The USA tests a 5 megaton nuclear device at Amchitka Island in Alaska; it is the largest American underground nuclear explosion.

Sunday 7: The USSR's Duga early warning radar system is used for the first time. It is nicknamed the 'Russian Woodpecker' by amateur radio listeners, due to its repetitive tapping sound on the airwaves.

Duga radar masts at Chernobyl in the Ukraine.

November 1971

Monday 8: Led Zeppelin release their fourth studio album, which is untitled. It goes on to become the best selling album of 1972.

Tuesday 9: John List, a 46 year old accountant from Westfield, New Jersey, goes on the run after murdering his wife, mother and three children. He is not apprehended until 1989.

Wednesday 10: The US senate approves a treaty to return the island of Okinawa, occupied since 1945, to Japanese control.

Thursday 11: 15 people are killed in Kawasaki, Japan, when a test on flooding effects causes a landslide.

Friday 12: President Nixon announces that 45,000 American troops will be withdrawn from Vietnam by February 1972.

Saturday 13: Mariner 9 becomes the first spacecraft to successfully enter Mars orbit.

Sunday 14: Pope Shenouda III of Alexandria, primate of the Coptic church, is enthroned.

Monday 15: Intel launches the first commercially available computer microprocessor, the Intel 4004. The chip allows the much smaller personal computers of the 1970s to be developed.

The Intel 4004 microprocesssor with its inventor, Federico Faggin.

November 1971

An Indian Army *Vijayant* tank used in the Indo-Pakistani War.

Tuesday 16: The British government begins an enquiry into the use of severe interrogation techniques by the army in Northern Ireland.

Wednesday 17: English actress and film star Gladys Cooper (*Now, Voyager*) dies aged 82.

Thursday 18: American air support is increased in Cambodia as communist troops close in on the capital, Pnomh Penh.

Friday 19: The Disney Fort Wilderness Resort opens in Orlando, Florida.

The veteran British actress Gladys Cooper dies on 17 November.

Saturday 20: 48 people are killed in a bridge collapse in Rio de Janeiro, Brazil.

Sunday 21: The 1971 Indo-Pakistani War begins.

Monday 22: Britain's worst mountaineering disaster occurs when five school pupils and their instructor die during a blizzard on Cairn Gorm in the Scottish Highlands.

November 1971

Tuesday 23: 197 Indian troops are killed during fighting on the Indian/East Pakistan border.

Artist's impression of hijacker 'D.B. Cooper'.

Wednesday 24: The only unsolved case of air hijack in US history takes place as a man known only as D.B. Cooper demands $200,000 and a parachute after taking a plane hostage at Seattle airport. After the ransom is paid, Cooper forces the crew to take off again and jumps out with the parachute, never to be seen again.

The Kinks release their album *Muswell Hillbillies*, named after the suburb of Muswell Hill, London N10, where they grew up.

Thursday 25: Pakistan announces that 1000 Indian soldiers have been killed in the first days of fighting in the Indo-Pakistan War.

Friday 26: The rock group Yes releases its album *Fragile*. It is the first to feature their new keyboard player, Rick Wakeman.

Saturday 27: The USSR's Mars 2 probe lands on the surface of the Red Planet. Although it is the first man made object to reach Mars, it malfunctions during descent and all communication is lost.

Sunday 28: The Prime Minister of Jordan, Wasfi al-Tal, is assassinated in Cairo by Palestinian militants.

Monday 29: The Pink Floyd single *One Of Those Days* is released in the UK.

Tuesday 30: Following British withdrawal, Iranian forces seize the newly independent islands of Abu Musa and the Greater and Lesser Tunbs in the Persian Gulf.

December 1971

Wednesday 1: In order to slow inflation, the US senate votes to extend price controls until 1973.

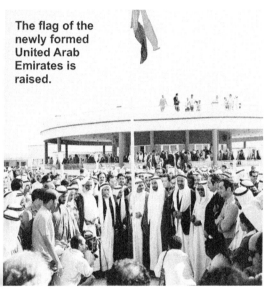

The flag of the newly formed United Arab Emirates is raised.

Thursday 2: Following independence from Britain, the United Arab Emirates (UAE) is founded by the seven Sheikdoms of the Persian Gulf.

The USSR's Mars 3 probe successfully lands on the planet's surface, but communication is lost before any information can be received.

Friday 3: Goodwill Zwelithini kaBhekuzulu is crowned King of the Zulus in a ceremony attended by 20,000 people in Nongoma, South Africa.

Saturday 4: The Montreux Casino in Montreux, Switzerland, burns down after a fire starts during a Frank Zappa concert. The incident inspires the Deep Purple song, *Smoke On The Water.*

15 people are killed when Ulster loyalists bomb McGurk's Bar in Belfast, Northern Ireland.

Sunday 5: The Taj Mahal is camouflaged to prevent bomb attacks as fighting intensifies in the Indo-Pakistan War.

Monday 6: Autotrain, the USA's first motor-rail service opens to transport motor cars and their passengers between Lorton, Virginia and Sanford, Florida.

December 1971

Tuesday 7: Wings, the band led by former Beatle Paul McCartney, releases its first album, *Wild Life*.

Wednesday 8: Sean Russell, an off duty member of the Ulster Defence Regiment, is shot dead by the IRA in Belfast. He is the first Roman Catholic soldier to be killed in the Troubles.

Thursday 9: The Indian Army surrounds Dacca as East Pakistan troops become outnumbered.

Friday 10: John Lennon and Yoko Ono perform at a rally at the University of Michigan in protest against the imprisonment of the poet John Sinclair on drugs charges.

Saturday 11: Indian troops continue their surge into East Pakistan, taking 3000 Pakistani troops prisoner.

Sunday 12: John Barnhill, former Deputy Speaker of the Northern Ireland parliament, is murdered by IRA gunmen at his home in Strabane, County Tyrone.

John Lennon and Yoko Ono perform in MIchigan on 10 December.

December 1971

Lieutenant General Amir Niazi, Governor of East Pakistan, signs the instrument of surrender to Indian forces on 16 December.

Monday 13: Demonstrations take place outside the US Embassy in New Delhi, as protestors accuse America of pro-Pakistani bias following its decision to cease ammunition sales to India.

Tuesday 14: As Indian forces close in, Pakistani authorities execute over 200 people considered to be supporters of Bangladeshi independence.

Wednesday 15: Pakistan's Foreign Minister walks out of the UN Security Council's meeting in protest over the council's treatment of his country during the war against India.

The US senate proposes a bill to allow draft dodgers who have moved to Canada to return to the USA if they agree to three years' community service.

Thursday 16: Pakistan's forces surrender to India, ending the Indo-Pakistan war and securing the independence of Bangladesh.

David Bowie releases his fourth studio album, *Hunky Dory*.

Friday 17: Sean Connery returns to the role of James Bond, as *Diamonds Are Forever* receives its US premiere.

December 1971

Sean Connery as James Bond in a scene from *Diamonds Are Forever.*

Saturday 18: For only the second time in its history, the US Dollar is devalued, by approximately 11%, in order to boost international trade.

Sunday 19: Stanley Kubrick's controversial dystopian film, A *Clockwork Orange,* starring Malcolm McDowell, premieres in New York City.

Monday 20: The film studio magnate Roy O. Disney, older brother of Walt Disney, dies aged 78.

The first issue of left-wing feminist magazine *Ms*, edited by Gloria Steinem, is published as an insert in *New York* magazine.

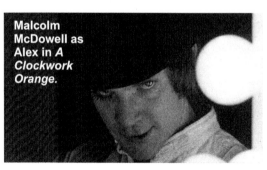

Malcolm McDowell as Alex in *A Clockwork Orange.*

Tuesday 21: The Austrian ambassador, Kurt Waldheim, succeeds Burma's U Thant as Secretary General of the United Nations.

December 1971

Canada's Prime Minister Justin Trudeau is born on 25 December.

Wednesday 22: US President Richard Nixon formally announces an extension of his 'Nixon Shock' package of price controls to reduce inflation until 1973.

Thursday 23: The US State Department announces that comedian Bob Hope is to make an unofficial attempt to broker the release of American prisoners of war in North Vietnam.

Friday 24: Juliane Koepcke, 17, is the sole survivor of an air crash in the Amazon jungle, in which 90 passengers die. Miss Koepcke walks for 11 days before finding rescuers.

Saturday 25: Justin Trudeau, 23rd Prime Minister of Canada, is born in Ottawa, Ontario.

Sunday 26: Reports emerge from Australia of sightings of the 'Nullarbor Nymph', a scantily clad young woman living wild amongst kangaroos in the remote Nullarbor Desert. A media storm ensues but in 1972 the story is revealed as a hoax.

Austria's Kurt Waldheim becomes Secretary General of the United Nations on 21 December.

December 1971

Golda Meir.

Pete Duel.

Monday 27: Vietnam veterans stage an anti-war protest at the Statue of Liberty; other demonstrations take place at Travis Air Force Base and in Philadelphia.

Tuesday 28: Further anti-war protests take place in the USA, with 80 arrests at Washington's Lincoln Memorial, as the USAF steps up aerial bombardment in North Vietnam in an effort to bring the war to a close.

Wednesday 29: Britain announces the withdrawal of most of its forces from its former colony of Malta; the last troops leave in 1979.

Thursday 30: Israel's Prime Minister Golda Meir concludes a state visit to the USA.

Friday 31: Actor Pete Duel, famous for his role in the TV western serial *Alias Smith and Jones*, commits suicide aged 31.

Birthday Notebooks
...a great alternative to a card.

Handy 60 page ruled notebooks with a significant event from the
year heading each page.

Available from Montpelier Publishing at Amazon.

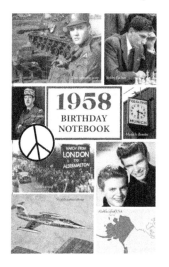

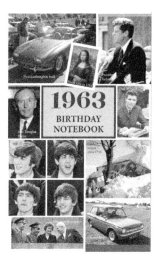

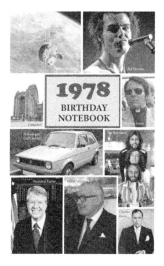

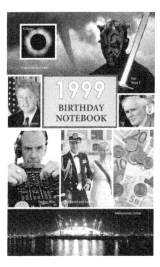

Printed in Great Britain
by Amazon